T030647

how to be a wildflower

a field guide by katie daisy

CHRONICLE BOOKS
SAN FRANCISCO

To
Heather Bee,
the most wild
of flowers.

CONTENTS

introduction

I meander down the path between cornfield and fence, my daily ritual. The sun lights up the wild daisies growing along fence posts while red-winged blackbirds sing hymns to the meadow. This is Lindenwood, Illinois, and I am a wildflower.

I'm a single stem of wheat, swaying in the sun.

A hummingbird drinking from a columbine plant.

A fluttering tadpole, stretching her new legs in the pond.

Lindenwood is a town of 505 people nestled on the banks of the Kilbuck Creek. It was my home ten years ago, and remains home to me always. When you're a child in a Lindenwood summer, time does not exist. The days are long, full of wonder, and the setting sun is not a marker of a day's work done but an invitation to explore the night. The yard becomes dappled with fireflies, the sky spread with the brightest of constellations, and the distant coyote howl becomes a lullaby to it all.

I've grown up in nature. My relationship with it has shaped who I've become, and continues still. Since age ten I've been grasping onto that smell of the sun-drenched cornfield and the touch of a warm, gentle breeze on my cheek.

I weave the muddy creek and Queen Anne's lace
through my hair, becoming one with the landscape
I hold so dear. In the same way, I attempt to
take that wonderment of a rural afternoon in
Lindenwood and lace it into every choice of my
adult life. I take the prairie with me everywhere
I go, into every new adventure. Lindenwood is an
actual place on the map, but it will always be
something more to me.

While I now live some two thousand miles away, in
a very different part of the country, I have found
a way to venture back to this idyllic land whenever
I need to. I remember the eyes I had as a child
and how easily they perceived the magic of the world.
I remember that I still have those eyes and can
still see the magic. And I find again a world of
wonders, as full of magic now as it has ever been.

This is a book that can help you find this truth, this magic in the world, in you. It can help you see it when it is hidden, to take hold of it while it is flying by, and to know what to do with it when you've got it. When it is forgotten, this book can remind you that it is still there.

This book is a field guide. It is best used in the field—under a giant willow tree, in a dew-kissed garden, or on a train ride down the California coast. In its pages you'll find inspirations of many kinds—things to do, things to make, places to go, places to stay, quotes, meditations, and guides to flora and fauna, clouds, and other things. It will serve you well through many years and many adventures. It is a book meant to be lovingly, yet fearlessly, used. Throw it in your bag with all the other adventure things, or tie it up with string and sling it over your shoulder. Write in it, and draw things. Pick green bits and pretty things and keep them inside, pressed between your favorite pages.

all good
things are
WILD
and
FREE

Henry David Thoreau

In each new day, wherever you may be, there is always waiting for you some beautiful discovery. The more you go in search, the more you find that every day will have at least one moment where the beauty is simply and abundantly clear. In that moment your eyes will open—and the beauty becomes a part of you, as you have opened your heart to it. Then you'll find that each day is stitched of such moments. You'll begin to gather these beautiful things and stitch them together yourself, finding life itself a patchwork quilt of beauty. It is waiting to be found, to be made. It waits for you.

So love,
look with eyes for seeing beauty,
and get out into it.

katie daisy.

Tomorrow to FRESH WOODS and PASTURES NEW

JOHN MILTON

a note on safety

Dear explorers, please be aware: It can be a wild and dangerous world out there. This is, of course, a part of why we love it so. May common sense and intuition be your constant companions—especially when adventuring alone. Leave a note, let someone know, take your phone just in case. Use a careful step on wet logs and river rocks. Watch out for sharp sticks and sharp-toothed animals. Carry water, and a flashlight at night. Don't be fearful of going where you've never been; this is half the point! Keep an eye on where the sun hangs, and take note of landmarks—rivers, roads, and things like that. Go with preparedness, awareness, caution, and joy.

"May your trails be
crooked, winding,
   lonesome, dangerous,
 leading to the most
     amazing view."
      —Edward Abbey

AFOOT AND
LIGHT-HEARTED
I TAKE TO
THE OPEN ROAD,
HEALTHY, FREE,
THE WORLD
BEFORE ME.

—WALT
WHITMAN

wanderlunch

- peach
- avocado
- baguette
- honey stick
- wedge of cheese
- thermos of tea
- piece of dark chocolate
- handful of almonds

Climb the mountains
and get their good tidings.
Nature's peace will flow into you as sunshine
flows into trees. The winds **will** blow their own
freshness into you, and the storms
their energy, while cares will
drop off like autumn leaves.

—John Muir

ADVENTURE THINGS

- compass
- pocket knife
- writing pen or pencil
- small notebook
- water canteen
- warm hat & sweater
- rain jacket
- flashlight or headlamp
- phone &/or camera
- bandanna
- strong string
- thermos for coffee or tea
- survival kit

going
to the
mountains
is going
home

-muir

MAGICAL PLACES TO·VISIT

- Take a day trip to Max Patch in North Carolina. Fly a kite across the grassy slopes.

- Hike through Effigy Mounds in Iowa and camp on the banks of the Mississippi.

- Look for the Mystery Lights in Marfa, Texas.

Take a summer drive with the windows down
to Illinois's Nachusa Grasslands.

Comb through thousands of treasures at
Glass Beach in Fort Bragg, California.

Devour a book among the redwoods at the
Henry Miller Memorial Library in Big Sur.

Back float in Austin's Barton Springs on
an early August morning.

Look for bears in the Boundary Waters Canoe
Area Wilderness in Minnesota.

Have a picnic by night around a bonfire at
Rockaway Beach on the Oregon Coast.

Drink homemade sarsaparilla at the "Rendez-
vous" in Prairie du Chien, Wisconsin.

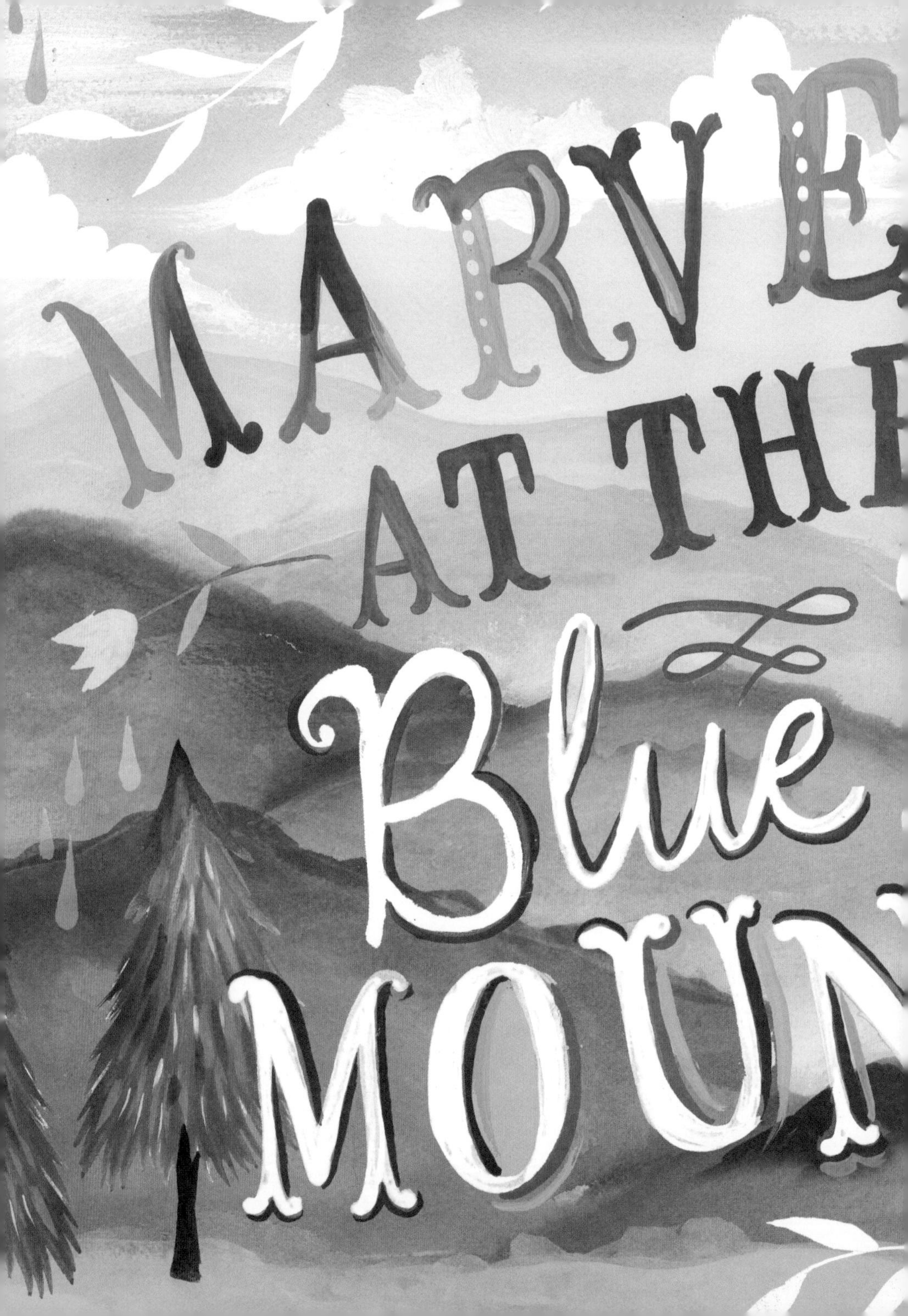
MARVE
AT TH
Blue
MOU

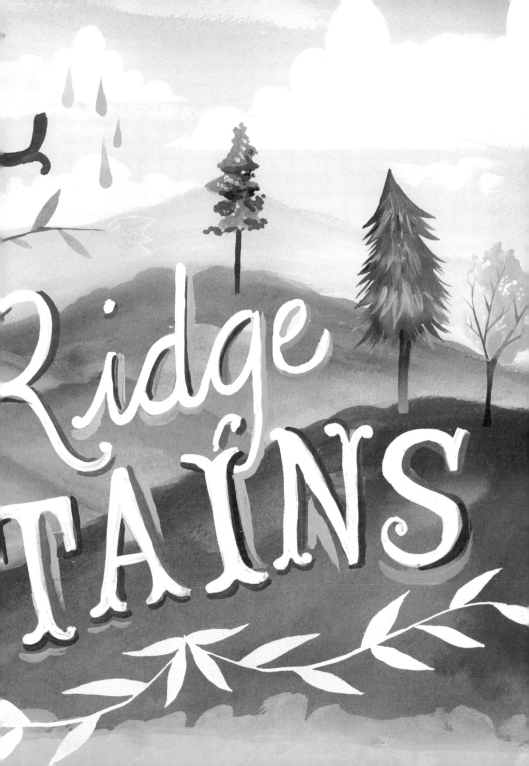

explore these NATIONAL FORESTS

Superior – MN
Deschutes – OR
Helena – MT
Sequoia – CA
Sierra – CA
Pisgah – NC

comb these
NATIONAL
SEASHORES
AND LAKESHORES

Canaveral — FL
Point Reyes — CA
Apostle Islands — WI
Pictured Rocks — MI
Indiana Dunes — IN

DAYDREAM UNDER

GIANT SEQUOIAS

POISONOUS PLANTS

Poison Ivy

Narcissus

Poison
Sumac

Lily
of the
Valley

Poison
Oak

STAY IN
A YURT
ON THE
OCEAN

Camping Checklist

- Tent
- Sleeping bag
- Pillow
- Hammock
- Warm clothes
- Boots
- Rain poncho
- First aid kit
- Toiletries
- Water bottle
- Hat
- Map
- Binoculars
- Pots and pans
- Utensils

- Natural insect repellent
- Firewood
- Matches
- Water
- Food
- Aluminum foil
- Cooler
- Paper towels
- Beach towel
- Swimsuit
- Backpack
- Sunglasses
- Whistle
- Lantern
- Rope
- Utility knife

HOW·TO PURIFY WATER

Collect water from flowing sources such as rivers whenever possible, and do not collect near, or downstream from, known animal homes.

You can prefilter your water with a close-knit cloth such as a bandanna. Several layers of cloth work best. Scoop the water holding cloth by the corners, then bring corners together to form a bag, and strain into a container. This will remove any dirt and other visible particles, though not all unseen elements that could be harmful.

The easiest way to ensure purification is to boil the previously filtered water over a fire or camp stove. Bring the water to a rolling boil and let it go a full ten minutes before removing from the heat and allowing to cool.

TAKE
CROSS
ROAD

44

A COUNTRY TRIP

DRIVE DOWN HIGHWAY 1 WITH THE WINDOWS OPEN.

FEEL THE SALT AIR & WARM BREEZE ON YOUR SKIN.

47

GET LOST IN AN UNFAMILIAR TOWN

WALNUT, IOWA

YACHATS, OREGON

HARRISON, MAINE

WEAVERVILLE,
NORTH CAROLINA

LINDENWOOD, ILLINOIS

MENDOCINO, CALIFORNIA

FALL CREEK, WISCONSIN

take a

FULL
MOON
HIKE

let it light
your path

Common Hazel

White Willow

Western Hemlock

European Larch

Wild Cherry

Coastal Redwood

Aspen

Sycamore

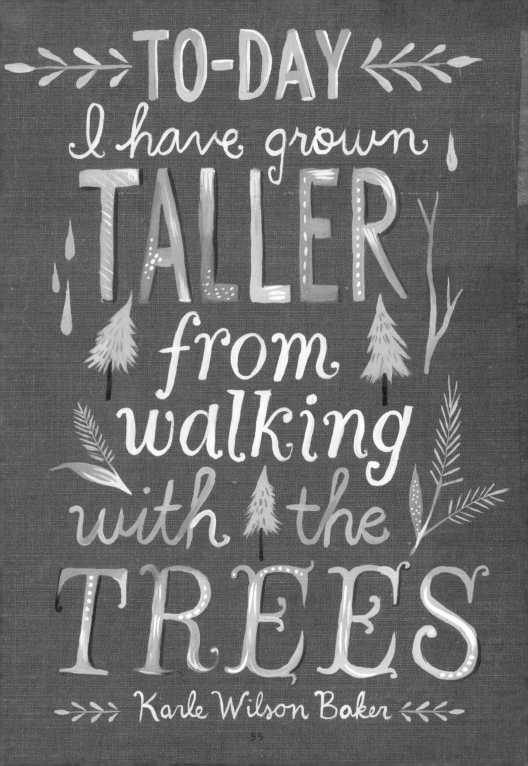

TO-DAY
I have grown
TALLER
from
walking
with the
TREES
Karle Wilson Baker

HOT SPRINGS
to visit

Bathing in hot springs offers wonderful benefits for the mind, body, and spirit. Soak in the warm pools listed below to reduce stress, relieve pain, and detoxify your body.

1. Bagby Hot Springs, OR
2. Strawberry Park Hot Springs, CO
3. Chena Hot Springs, AK
4. Travertine Hot Springs, CA
5. Gila Hot Springs, NM
6. Fifth Water Hot Springs, UT

if there is MAGIC on this PLANET it is contained in WATER

—Loren Eiseley

TAKE A
CANOE TRIP THAT
CREEPS INTO THE
NIGHT,
THEN
SET UP
CAMP
ON SHORE.

paper birch

know these LEAVES

black walnut

sugar maple

honey locust

cottonwood

FUNGI

HONEY
WAXCAP

AMANITA

OLD
MAN
OF THE
WOODS

For visual enjoyment only—some are poisonous

SHAGGY PARASOL

MOREL

CHANTERELLE

I
must
HAVE
FLOWERS
ALWAYS,
ALWAYS.
-monet

MOTHS

Io

Imperial

Luna

Cecropia

EDIBLE PLANTS

Asparagus

Wild Onion

Fiddleheads

Violets

Dandelion

Garlic
Mustard

FIND A
FIELD OF
DANDELIONS.
MAKE 100
WISHES.

Red-winged Blackbird

Oriole

Yellow Warbler

Purple Finch

Goldfinch

Bluejay

KNOW THESE BIRDS

grow a garden with cosmos, daisies, poppies & humming-birds.

know these
WILDFLOWERS

California
Poppy

Cosmos

Black-eyed
Susan

Wild Daisy

Purple Coneflower

Queen Anne's
Lace

Buttercup

Bachelor's
Button

85

Common
Wild Rose

There are FLOWERS EVERYWHERE for those who want TO SEE THEM

-HENRI MATISSE-

press your

flowers here

cirrus

cirrostratus

altostratus

stratocumulus

cumulus

stratus

nimbostratu

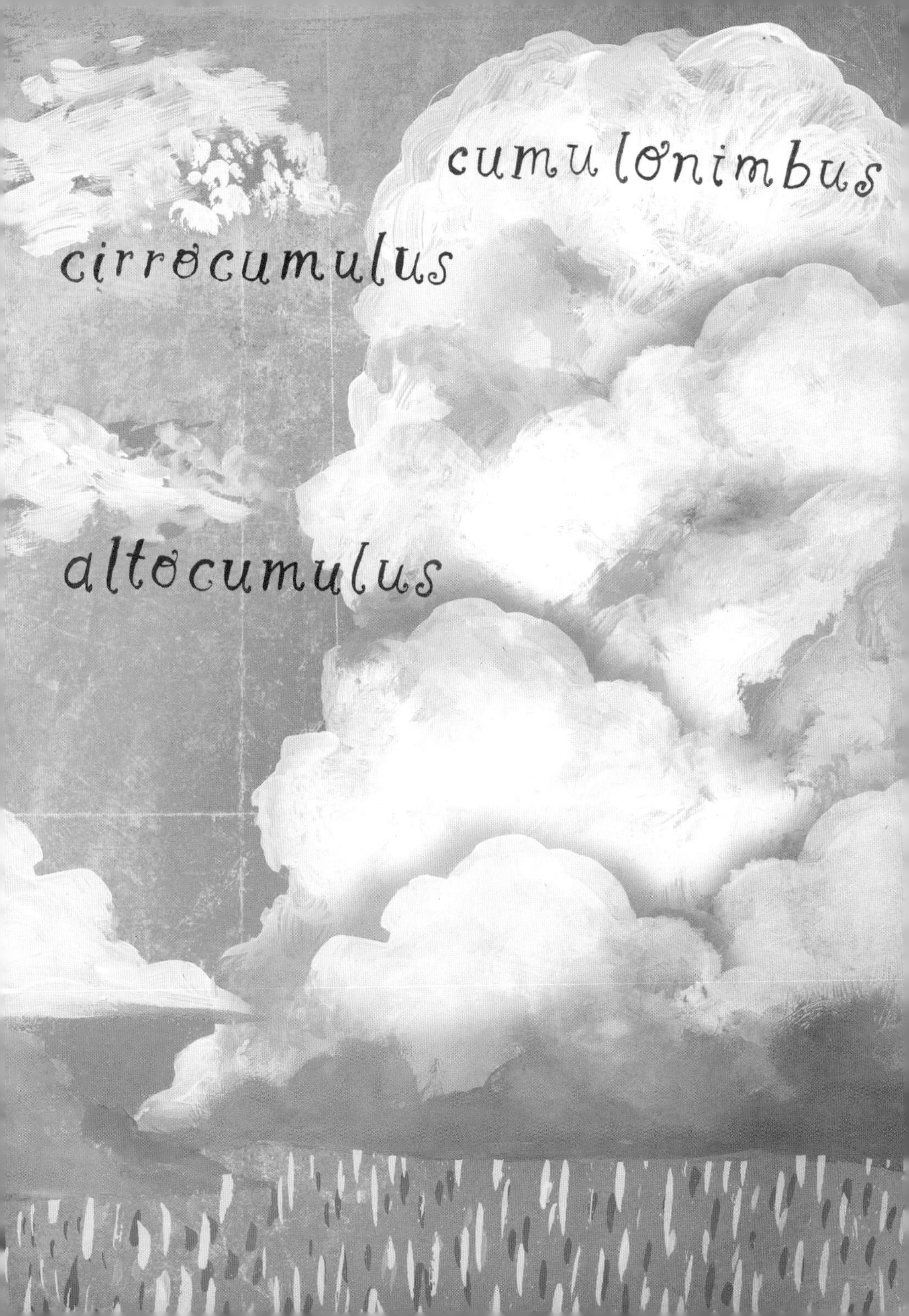
cumulonimbus
cirrocumulus
altocumulus

MY SOUL is MADE of meadow flowers

Gather:

A basketful of wildflowers and plants of various sizes. Be sure the stems are bendable.

Instructions:

1. Group flowers according to stem length.

2. Take the flowers with the shorter stems and put them in small bundles. Secure them by using one or two of the long-stemmed variety to tie the clusters together, as if using twine. Tie the knots gently so the stems don't break.

3. Finish enough bundles to create a circlet that, when the clusters overlap, sits nicely on the top of your head.

4. In the same manner as you secured the individual bundles, use the long-stemmed flowers to lash them all together.

This process can require a certain dexterity of the fingers and might be frustrating. Don't give up! Creativity often requires patience.

MAKE A
WILDFLOWER
CROWN

spend
an hour
looking for
four-leaf
clovers

press them in these pages

There is pleasure in
the pathless woods
There is a rapture
on the lonely shore
There is society
where none intrudes
By the deep sea
and music in its roar
I love not man the
less but Nature more
—Lord Byron

KEEP
BEES

SOME BENEFITS OF KEEPING BEES:

- ♥ HONEY
- ♥ CONNECTION TO NATURE
- ♥ BEESWAX
- ♥ EDUCATION
- ♥ THE BEST POLLINATORS

KEEP CHICKENS

Love and eggs
are best when
they are fresh.
Russian Proverb

Explore
a Tidepool

Octopus

Surfgrass

Mussel

Starfish

Sculpin

Anemone

Coral

Urchin

Crab

105

gather unlike frien

lavender
SIMPLE SYRUP

Use this syrup in your summer cocktails, iced coffee, or lemonade!

1 cup (240 ml) pure water
2 cups (400 g) organic cane sugar
4 Tbsp (60 g) fresh lavender

Heat the water until boiling and add the cane sugar.

Simmer for 20 minutes, stirring often, until the sugar dissolves. Turn off the heat but do not remove from the stove top.

Remove the petals from the lavender, discarding the stems.

While the syrup is still hot, crush
the lavender in the palms of your
hands and add petals to the liquid.

Cover and let stand for an addi-
tional 10 minutes or longer to draw
the lavender flavors into the syrup.

Use a muslin cloth to strain the
lavender buds out of syrup, and pour
directly into a glass bottle or jar.

Cover and refrigerate to extend the
life of the syrup.

stay close
to anything
that makes
you glad you
are alive
—HAFIZ—

Pink skies
Forest waterfalls
Roadside poppies
Bats swooping at dusk
Barn kittens
Night swimming
Iced coffee from a drinking jar
Sparklers
A summertime romance
Rubbing sage between your fingers
Fireflies emerging from the grass in twilight
Dewy grass and bare feet
Fresh basil
The perfect peach

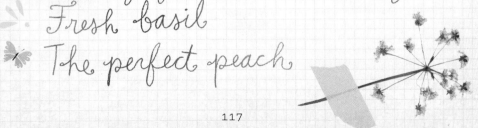

* Making a tepee and spending the entire day there with books
* Adding chamomile to cocktails
* Allowing yourself to be free
* A baby smiling at you
* A tree that grows over the river
* Running through a field
* Muddy feet and messy hair
* An outdoor shower
* The best hug you've ever received
* The greenest pasture you've ever seen

It is
the sweet,
simple things
of life
which are
the real ones
after all

—Laura Ingalls Wilder

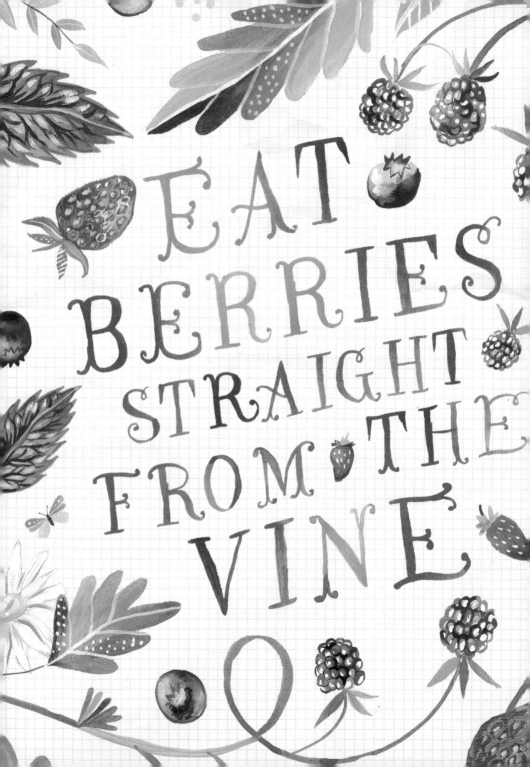

CHEERILY-CHEERILY-CHEER-UP!
ROBIN
BIRDIE-BIRDIE-BIRDIE
CARDINAL
EASTERN TOWHEE
Learn to identify birdsongs

CHICKA-DEE-DEE-DEE!
CHICKADEE
DRINK-YOUR-TEEEE!
TURR-TURLEE-TURLEE!
EASTERN BLUEBIRD

THE

IN

YOU

Hughes

125

WALK DOWN A DIRT PATH AT SUNSET

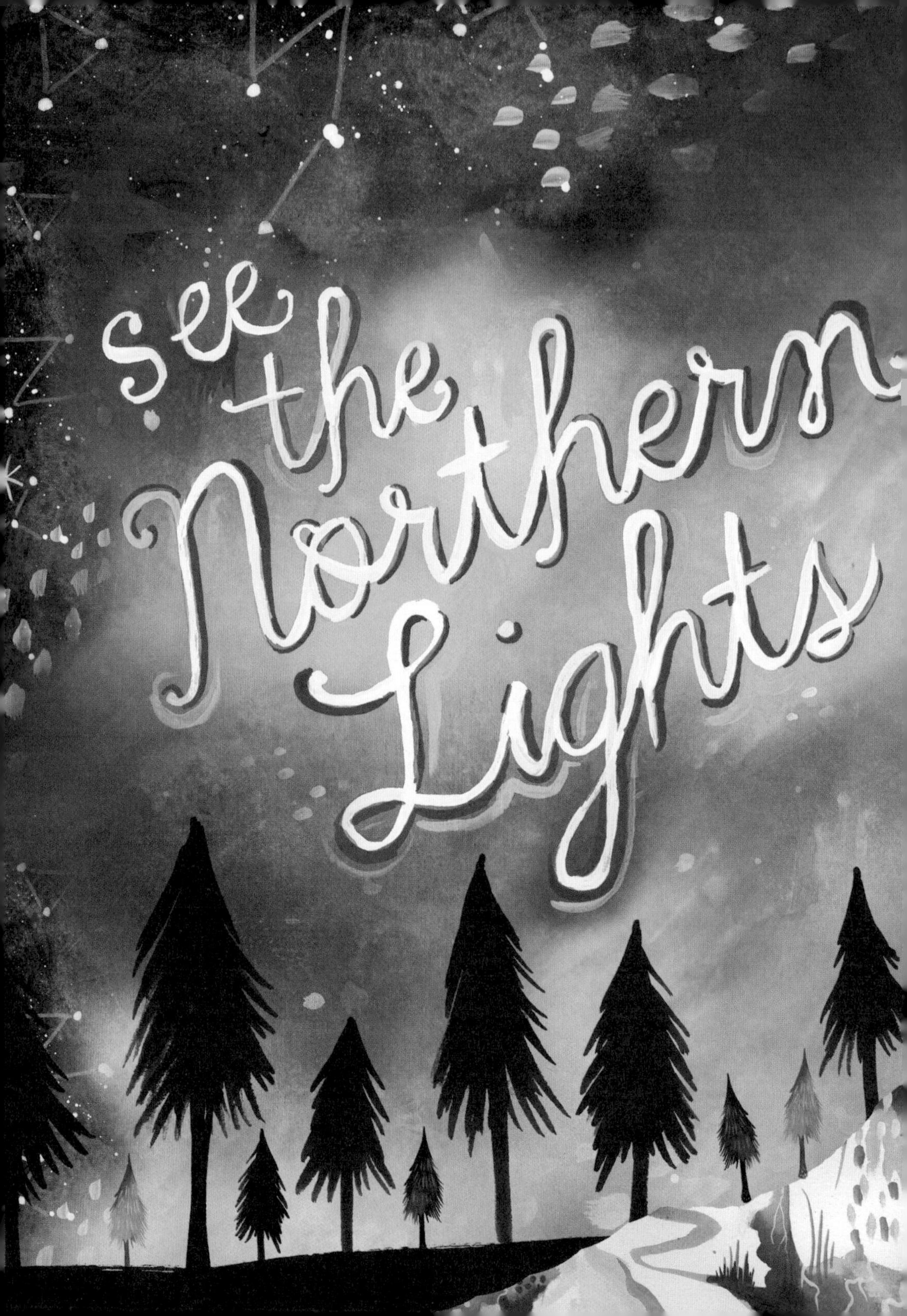
see the Northern Lights

Take a SUMMER MINERAL BATH with the windows open

2 cups (480 ml) milk or buttermilk
1 cup (240 ml) honey
1 cup (270 g) pink Himalayan salt
A handful or two of fresh or
    dried rose petals & buds
A handful of fresh or dried
    chamomile flowers

Pour the milk, honey, and
salt into warm running
bathwater. Swirl the water
around to mix everything well.
When the tub is full, sprinkle in
the roses and chamomile flowers.
Sink in, exhale, and soak for 15
to 30 minutes. This bath will
leave your skin feeling soft
and smooth, detoxify your
body, and invite peace
and relaxation.

She smelled of SUN and DAISIES with a hint of RIVER WATER

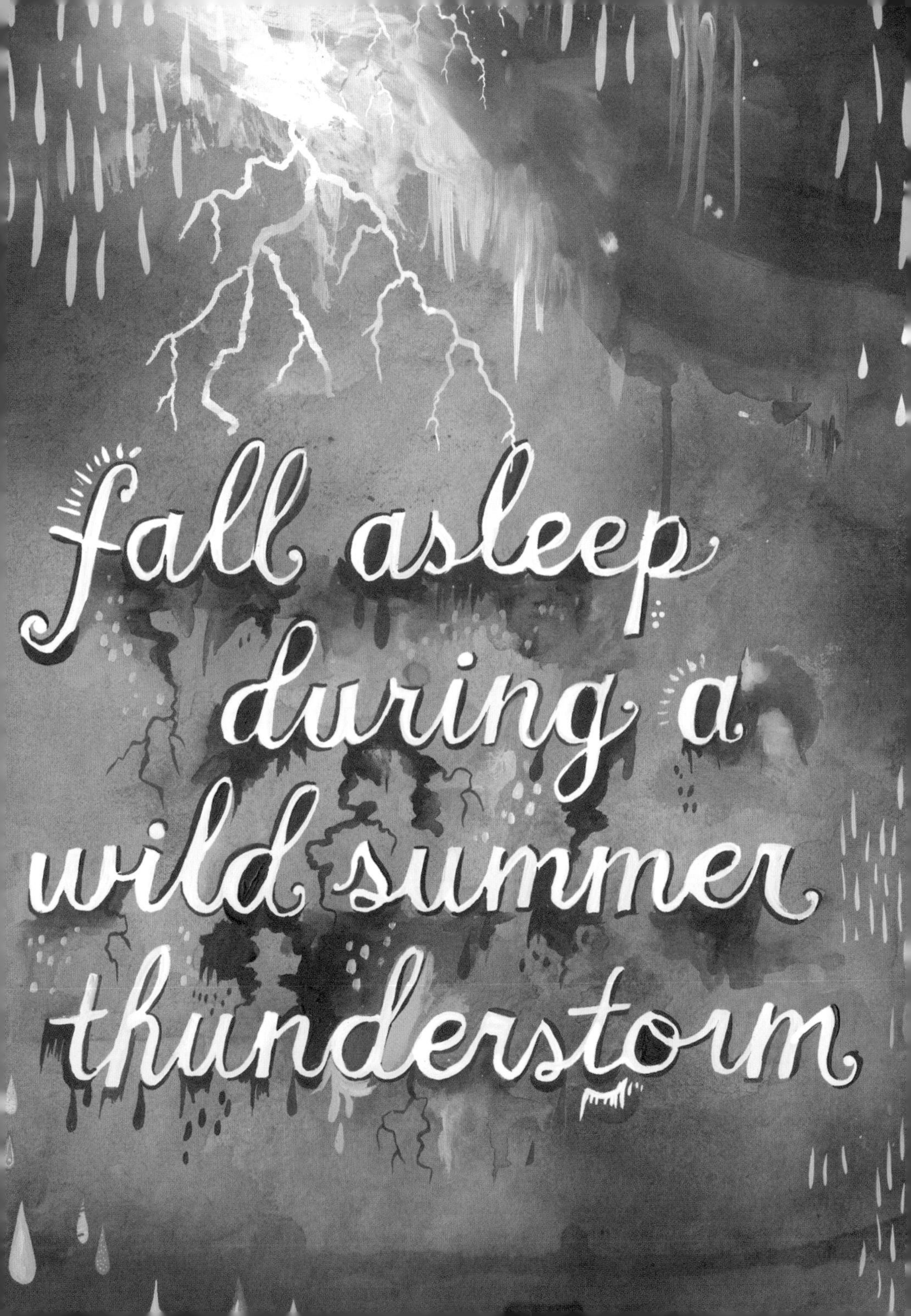
fall asleep during a wild summer thunderstorm

Cover Me in

hang your
clothes on the line.
they'll be infused with
sun & breeze
& birdsong

wear a SHEER & GAUZY DRESS in the afternoon BREEZE

Marie in the Meadow

Johann Trojan

Edwin Kunz

1. Ma — rie in the mead-ow, In the mead-ow Ma — rie, All the flow-ers and
2. Oh, I am so wor-ried, I've lost my Ma — rie; She's lost in the

grass-es are tal — ler than she.
clo — ver, Oh, where can she be?

3. But who is it sitting 'mid the flowers so bright,
The harebells, the buttercups, the star daisies white?

4. This can't be a flower, a little head I see, —
I've found her, I've found her, I've found my Marie!

stumble
upon a
farm stand
in the
middle of
nowhere

Make a
STRAWBERRY PIE
from scratch

CRUST

2½ cups (300 g) organic, all-purpose flour
1 Tbsp organic cane sugar
1 tsp salt
1 cup (220 g) unsalted butter, cubed & chilled
½ cup (120 ml) very cold water

Blend the flour, sugar, and salt together in
a large bowl. Use your fingertips to work
the butter into the mixture until the larg-
est pieces of butter are slightly bigger
than your thumbnail. Pour in the water and
mix with a wooden spoon or spatula until
the dough becomes a single mass, then knead
with your hands several times and form into
a ball. Divide the dough into two equal
parts, wrap each portion in plastic wrap,
and chill for at least one hour.

FILLING

2 cups (400 g) fresh strawberries
½ cup (120 ml) water
½ cup (100 g) organic cane sugar
Juice of 1 lemon
Handful of fresh basil leaves, minced
Pinch of freshly ground cinnamon

ASSEMBLE & BAKE

Thoroughly wash the strawberries and cut half of them into thumbnail sized pieces. Place in a pan over medium heat with a very small splash of water, then pour the sugar over the strawberries and cover. Stir occasionally, adding small amounts of water and lemon juice to keep from sticking to the pan. Once the strawberries have cooked down and their juices begin to thicken, add the basil and remove from the heat. Keep covered.

Cut the remaining strawberries in half and place them in a small bowl. Add the cinnamon, and shake.

Remove the chilled dough and roll
each part out on a floured sur-
face until it's about ¼ inch (6 mm)
thick. Place one disk into a 9-inch
(23 cm) pie pan, then gently press
into the bottom of the pan without tear-
ing the dough. Place the halved strawberries
into your crust, then pour the strawberry
mixture from the pan over them. Cover with
the second piece of dough and crimp the
edges all around the pie pan so that it
forms a bond with the bottom crust. Make
four symmetrical cuts in the top, in any
pattern you choose, which will allow the pie
to vent while baking. Place on the center
rack in the oven and cook at 450°F (230°C)
for about 12 minutes or until the crust
turns golden brown around the edges. Remove
and allow to cool slightly before cutting.
Serve hot or refrigerate for at least 30
minutes to serve chilled.

RHUBARB ELIXIR

2 large stalks organic rhubarb
½ of a large cucumber
⅓ cup (85 g) organic cane sugar
Handful of fresh mint
Handful of fresh basil
Ice
4½ cups (1 L) sparkling mineral water
1 lime, quartered

Chop the rhubarb and cucumber into pieces
slightly larger than your thumb. Place the
rhubarb in a pot on the stove with just enough
water to cover, then pour the sugar over top.
Cook on medium-high heat, stirring occasionally,
until the sugar has dissolved entirely. Remove
from the heat, mash the rhubarb, and cool.

Divide the cucumber, mint, and basil equally
among four pint glasses. Add the rhubarb mixture to each glass, straining with a fork to
keep out the larger pieces. Muddle the ingre-
dients and add the desired amount of ice.
Top with mineral water, stir gently,
garnish with a lime
wedge and serve.

MOREL MUSHROOM & FIDDLEHEAD FERN OMELET

You can forage for wild fiddlehead ferns and morel mushrooms in the Northeastern wetlands during springtime. Morels are also common in the coniferous forests of the western states. (When picking wild mushrooms, please remember to always use a detailed identification guide! True morels often grow alongside false morels, which can be dangerous to eat.)

4 Tbsp (55 g) unsalted butter   Serves 2
6 to 8 rinsed morel mushrooms
Pinch of sea salt
6 to 8 fiddlehead ferns, blanched or washed
Splash of balsamic vinegar
Pinch of freshly ground peppercorns
3 large organic eggs
Splash of heavy cream

Melt half of the butter in a small saute pan over medium heat. Add the mushrooms and simmer for about 12 minutes or until the sauce thickens. Add the salt.

In a separate saucepan over medium heat, add the remaining butter and ferns. Bring to a simmer, then add the balsamic vinegar and peppercorns, and continue to cook for about 5 minutes. Set the ferns aside in a small bowl, leaving the saucepan on the stove top.

Whisk the eggs with the cream until they just begin to foam. Pour into the empty pan you used for the ferns and cook over medium heat. Once the edges begin to brown, flip the eggs and place the ferns in the center of the omelet. With both sides finished, place on a plate and fold in half. Pour the mushrooms over the top of the omelet. Serve while hot!

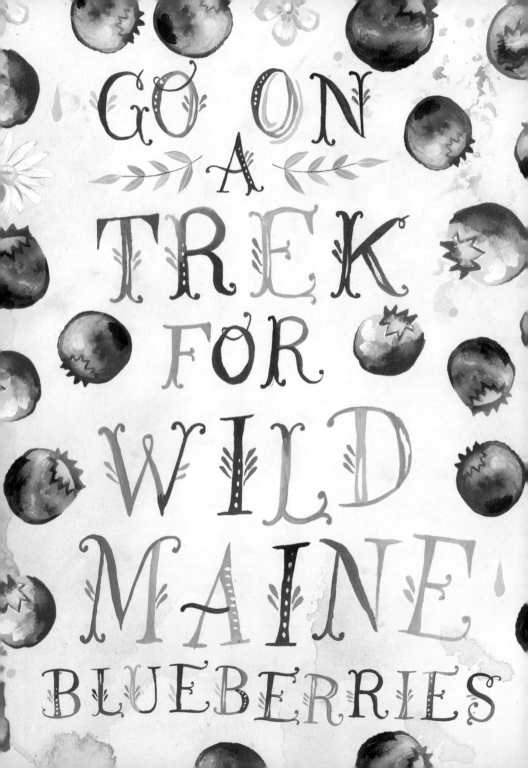

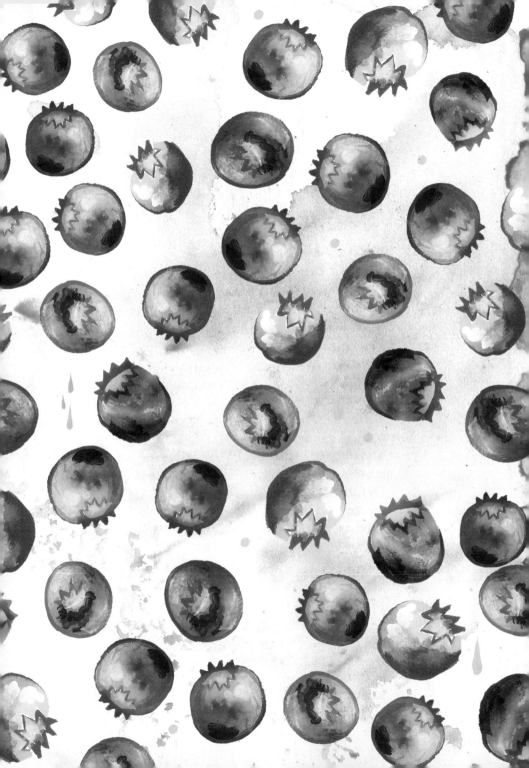

GIVE
ME THE
splendid
SILENT
SUN

with
ALL · HIS
BEAMS
FULL
dazzling

walt whitman

HOW TO EVOKE A DAYDREAM

Gather three or more of the following items:

    a cup of tea
    a journal
    fresh cut flowers
    a rainstorm
    old photographs
    your favorite book
    a wishing dandelion
    a crystal

1. Find a quiet spot (in a sunny meadow or in the shade of a tree).

2. Take several deep breaths to sink into the moment.

3. Gaze at your items for several minutes.

4. Close your eyes and drift away into a pleasant thought (a faraway place, a creative idea, a sweet memory).

5. Take another deep breath.

6. Stay awhile.

Make a NATURE MANDALA

The mandala originates in Eastern traditions dating back thousands of years. It is often created with intricate patterns of colored sand over the course of many days of meditation and ceremony. At the completion of the ritual, all the sand and colors of the painting are gathered together and poured into a body of flowing water. In this way, the mandala represents the impermanence of life and the fluid nature of the universe.

Create your own symbol of beauty and impermanence by using objects found in nature. Take a basket into the garden or forest. Gather many items that speak to your spirit (leaves, pinecones, seeds, flower petals, stones). Remember to be gentle on the earth—pick only what you need.

Find a location to create your mandala. A flat section of ground or beach works well. Start by putting one item down. This will be the center of your mandala. Encircle that item with other

natural materials, as pictured. You may alternate the
pattern by material, color, or shape. Continue this
process until you reach a desired size.

Be still for a while with the art you've just created. After meditating on the mandala for a good while,
destroy it! Scatter the petals in the air or throw the
materials into the river.

Ursa Major

Cassiopeia

know these
CONSTEL

Hercules

Keep these CRYSTALS nearby for their POWERS and PROTECTIONS:

Reduces stress,
protects from
negative forces
& energy.
An electric,
grounding stone.

BLACK
TOURMALINE

LABRADORITE

A magical
stone. Awakens your
psychic abilities, enhancing your
intuition and awareness. Protects
your aura from negativity.

ROSE QUARTZ

Stone of love (all types)— self love, family love, erotic love. Use to raise self-esteem & balance emotions. A peaceful, calming crystal.

CITRINE

Stone of abundance and manifestation. Expands imagination, creativity, and personal power.

TIGER'S EYE

A balancing stone. Protects during adventures. Brings wealth and prosperity.

FLUORITE

Stone of the spirit. Peaceful, calming crystal. Sets mind and emotions at ease. Aids in overcoming addiction.

AMETHYST

Absorbs negative energy. Opens the third eye. Protects on a psychic level and aids in stabilization. A meditative stone.

I have
LOVED
THE
STARS
TOO FONDLY
TO·BE Fearful
OF THE NIGHT

·sarah· williams·

SPIRIT ANIMALS

hummingbird

Throughout many ancient cultures, animal totems have been an important part of our connection to nature and finding our place in the world. Just as every person is unique, each spirit animal has different qualities, strengths, and personality characteristics.

fox

cleverness, quick wit, luck, charm, mischievousness

playfulness, intelligence, quirkiness, creativity

wanderlust, freedom, grace, guidance, endurance

horse

bear

joy,
love,
magic,
hope

strength,
bravery,
confidence,
power

Coming to know your spirit animal
can be a profound experience.
To begin this journey, spend time
alone among the creatures in nature.

otter

Keep a journal, taking note of
animal appearances in dreams and
works of art, and reflect upon your
own unique qualities. The ancients
believed that your animal finds you!
Keep watch and listen closely.

whale

wisdom,
peace,
gentleness,
depth of
emotion

Stand tall like a tree.
Plant your feet into the earth.
Sigh out loud.
Listen to the world that surrounds you.
Become one with your breath.
Watch your thoughts come & go like clouds floating by.
Sink into the present moment.
Just be.

Stand in the middle of
an open meadow or field.

Close your eyes and
take a deep breath.

Open your eyes to the sky,
stretch your arms wide,
and exclaim

"I AM ALIVE!"

Don't worry, the prairie will
never judge you and
the wildflowers will stand in
reverence of your bravery.

There
shall be
an eternal
SUMMER in the
grateful
HEART

-celia thaxter

where
do you
feel
most
alive?

Pick the first trail through
the thick part of the forest,
walk until you find a clearing or
a meadow. Imagine you've just
found your home.

What does
it look like?

With inexpressible delight you wade out into the grassy sun-lake, feeling yourself contained on one of Nature's most sacred chambers, withdrawn from the sterner influences of the mountains, secure from all intrusion, secure from yourself free in the universal beauty. And notwithstanding the scene is so impressively spiritual, and you seem dissolved in it yet everything about you is beating with warm terrestrial human love, delightfully substantial and familiar. —John Muir—

DESCRIBE THE MOST beautiful PLACE YOU'VE EVER BEEN

IF YOU'RE
A PAINTER,
TRY USING
WATER FROM
THE SEA
OR RIVER.
IT WILL ADD
A SWIRL OF
MAGIC TO
YOUR ART.

FIND A
SUN-WARMED
SPOT IN
THE WOODS
AND
DISSOLVE
INTO
THOREAU'S
WALDEN

Sometimes, in a summer
morning, having taken my
accustomed bath, I sat in my
sunny doorway from sunrise
till noon, rapt in a revery,
amidst the pines and hickories,
and sumachs, in undisturbed
solitude and stillness, while the
birds sing around or flitted
noiseless through the house,
until by the sun falling in at
my west window, or the noise
of some traveller's wagon on
the distant highway, I was
reminded of the lapse of time.

— Henry David Thoreau

GAZE UPON
A CLOUD-
FILLED SKY.
DRAW WHAT YOU SEE.

WEATHER FOLKLORE

The higher the clouds, the better the weather.

Clear moon, frost soon.

Rainbow at noon, more rain soon.

Cold is the night when the stars shine bright.

Trout jump high when a rain is nigh.

A sunshiny shower won't last an hour.

The daisy shuts its eye before rain.

If you see toadstools in the morning,
expect rain by evening.

Birds flying low, expect rain and a blow.

A single magpie in spring, foul weather will bring.

AND THE
BUMBLEBEE
SINGING
EVERY
SUMMER
THE SONGS
SUNG
A THOUSAND
YEARS AGO

-John Muir-

The trees began
to whisper
and the wind
began to roll
and in the wild
March morning
I heard them
call my soul

—Alfred Lord Tennyson

acknowledgments

To my love Elijah, for his support, affection, and delicious cooking. To my sweet baby Finn Orion, born in the middle of this project, who inspires me to look at the world with eyes of wonder. To my mom, Laurie, and my dad, Sam, for raising me with the utmost care & love in the fields, encouraging me to follow my heart and teaching me how important nature is for the soul. To my brother, Robby, an enormous inspiration who I will always see as an explorer, seeking to ever-fully understand the secrets of the universe. To Brian, for encouraging me with his work ethic, love for the land, and dedication to our family.

To my business mentor and dear friend, Betsy Cordes, for keeping me on track, and offering a never-ending flow of motivation, encouragement, and inspiration. Special thanks to Chuck Cordes for his work gathering permissions for the many quotations that appear in this book. Thank you to my dear friend Gabriel Edwards for helping me form ideas, edit, and stitch together my ramblings. To Alia, for her wisdom and knowledge surrounding self-care, to the Irwin family for their support and love. A very special thanks to Melanie for keeping my print shop afloat so I have time and freedom to paint.

I have so much gratitude for everyone who has contributed to my undying wanderlust and many adventures. You know who you are. Without you this book would not be possible.

Page 13: Quotation from preface to DESERT SOLITAIRE is reprinted by permission of Don Congdon Associates, Inc. © 1988 by Edward Abbey.

Page 57: Excerpt from THE IMMENSE JOURNEY: AN IMAGINATIVE NATURALIST EXPLORES THE MYSTERIES OF MAN AND NATURE by Loren Eiseley, copyright © 1946, 1950, 1951, 1953, 1955, 1956, 1957 by Loren Eiseley. Used by permission of Random House, an imprint and division of Random House LLC. All rights reserved.

Pages 62-63: Courtesy of the University of Texas Libraries, The University of Texas at Austin.

Page 87: © 2015 Succession H. Matisse / Artists Rights Society (ARS), New York.

Page 116: From the Penguin publication, THE GIFT, POEMS BY HAFIZ, copyright © 1999 Daniel Ladinsky and used with his permission.

Pages 124-125: "April Rain Song" from THE COLLECTED POEMS OF LANGSTON HUGHES by Langston Hughes, edited by Arnold Rampersad with David Roessel, Associate Editor, copyright © 1994 by the Estate of Langston Hughes. Used by permission of Alfred A. Knopf, an imprint of the Knopf Doubleday Publishing Group, a division of Penguin Random House LLC. All rights reserved.

Page 141: "Marie in the Meadow" from SING THROUGH THE DAY, © 1968 Plough Publishing House.

Pages 158-159: Excerpt from A SHADOW PASSES used by permission of The Royal Literary Fund, © 1918 Eden Phillpotts.

Page 201: Excerpt from JOHN OF THE MOUNTAINS, edited by Linnie Marsh Wolfe. Copyright 1938 by Wanda Muir Hanna; copyright renewed © 1966 by John Muir Hanna and Ralph Eugene Wolfe. Reprinted by permission of Houghton Mifflin Harcourt Publishing Company. All rights reserved.

Library of Congress Cataloging-in-Publication Data available.
ISBN: 978-1-4521-4268-5
Manufactured in China

20 19 18 17 16 15 14 13

Chronicle Books LLC
680 Second Street
San Francisco, CA 94107
www.chroniclebooks.com

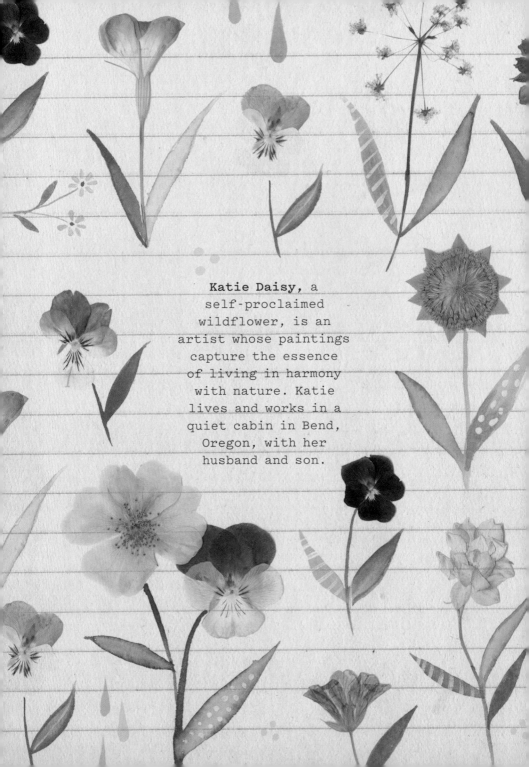

Katie Daisy, a
self-proclaimed
wildflower, is an
artist whose paintings
capture the essence
of living in harmony
with nature. Katie
lives and works in a
quiet cabin in Bend,
Oregon, with her
husband and son.